Navigating Your School Cafeteria and Convenience Store

Mason Crest
450 Parkway Drive, Suite D
Broomall, PA 19008
www.masoncrest.com

Printed and bound in the United States of America.

First printing
9 8 7 6 5 4 3 2 1

Series ISBN: 978-1-4222-2874-6
ISBN: 978-1-4222-2882-1
ebook ISBN: 978-1-4222-8944-0

The Library of Congress has cataloged the
        hardcopy format(s) as follows:

        Library of Congress Cataloging-in-Publication Data

Crockett, Kyle A.
    Navigating your school cafeteria and convenience store / Kyle A. Crockett.
        pages cm. – (Understanding nutrition: a gateway to physical & mental health)
    ISBN 978-1-4222-2882-1 (hardcover) – ISBN 978-1-4222-2874-6 (series) – ISBN 978-1-4222-8944-0 (ebook)
    1. Health behavior–Juvenile literature. 2. Nutrition–Juvenile literature. 3. School lunchrooms, cafeterias, etc.–Juvenile literature. 4. Convenience foods–Juvenile literature. I. Title.
    RA776.9.C76 2014
    613.2–dc23
                        2013009805

Produced by Vestal Creative Services.
www.vestalcreative.com

UNDERSTANDING NUTRITION:
A GATEWAY TO PHYSICAL AND MENTAL HEALTH

Navigating Your School Cafeteria and Convenience Store

KYLE A. CROCKETT

Mason Crest

CONTENTS

Introduction   6
1. Why Do Food Choices Matter?   9
2. Choices in the Cafeteria   19
3. Spending Wisely, Staying Healthy   35
Find Out More   46
Index   47
About the Author & Consultant and Picture Credits   48

INTRODUCTION

by Dr. Joshua Borus

There are many decisions to make about food. Almost everyone wants to "eat healthy"—but what does that really mean? What is the "right" amount of food and what is a "normal" portion size? Do I need sports drinks if I'm an athlete—or is water okay? Are all "organic" foods healthy? Getting reliable information about nutrition can be confusing. All sorts of restaurants and food makers spend billions of dollars trying to get you to buy their products, often by implying that a food is "good for you" or "healthy." Food packaging has unbiased, standardized nutrition labels, but if you don't know what to look for, they can be hard to understand. Magazine articles and the Internet seem to always have information about the latest fad diets or new "superfoods" but little information you can trust. Finally, everyone's parents, friends, and family have their own views on what is healthy. How are you supposed to make good decisions with all this information when you don't know how to interpret it?

The goal of this series is to arm you with information to help separate what is healthy from not healthy. The books in the series will help you think about things like proper portion size and how eating well can help you stay healthy, improve your mood, and manage your weight. These books will also help you take action. They will let you know some of the changes you can make to keep healthy and how to compare eating options.

Keep in mind a few broad rules:

- First, healthy eating is a lifelong process. Learning to try new foods, preparing foods in healthy ways, and focusing on the big picture are essential parts of that process. Almost no one can keep on a very restrictive diet for a long time or entirely cut out certain groups of foods, so it's best to figure out how to eat healthy in a way that's realistic for you by making a number of small changes.

- Second, a lot of healthy eating hasn't really changed much over the years and isn't that complicated once you know what to look for. The core of a healthy diet is still eating reasonable portions at regular meals. This should be mostly fruits and vegetables, reasonable amounts of proteins, and lots of whole grains, with few fried foods or extra fats. "Junk food" and sweets also have their place—they taste good and have a role in celebrations and other happy events—but they aren't meant to be a cornerstone of your diet!

- Third, avoid drinks with calories in them, beverages like sodas, iced tea, and most juices. Try to make your liquid intake all water and you'll be better off.

- Fourth, eating shouldn't be done mindlessly. Often people will munch while they watch TV or play games because it's something to do or because they're bored rather then because they are hungry. This can lead to lots of extra food intake, which usually isn't healthy. If you are eating, pay attention, so that you are enjoying what you eat and aware of your intake.

- Finally, eating is just one part of the equation. Exercise every day is the other part. Ideally, do an activity that makes you sweat and gets your heart beating fast for an hour a day—but even making small decisions like taking stairs instead of elevators or walking home from school instead of driving make a difference.

After you read this book, don't stop. Find out more about healthy eating. Choosemyplate.gov is a great Internet resource from the U.S. government that can be trusted to give good information; www.hsph.harvard.edu/nutritionsource is a webpage from the Harvard School of Public Health where scientists sort through all the data about food and nutrition and distill it into easy-to-understand messages. Your doctor or nurse can also help you learn more about making good decisions. You might also want to meet with a nutritionist to get more information about healthy living.

Food plays an important role in social events, informs our cultural heritage and traditions, and is an important part of our daily lives. It's not just how we fuel our bodies; it's also but how we nourish our spirit. Learn how to make good eating decisions and build healthy eating habits—and you'll have increased long-term health, both physically and psychologically.

So get started now!

1

Why Do Food Choices Matter?

Food is something you think about every day. Do you have time to eat breakfast? What should you eat for lunch? How much should you eat?

The answers to all these questions—and other questions like them—make up nutrition. Nutrition is all the ways you choose to eat food. Nutrition includes what you eat, when you eat, and how much you eat.

Food is way more than just something tasty you chew and swallow a few times a day. The food you choose to eat has a lot to do with the rest of your health. Your food choices affect how well your body and mind work, how you look, how you feel, and even how well you do in school and in sports.

Your goal should be *good* nutrition. Good nutrition will help you lead the best life you can. Healthy food choices will help you feel and look great!

Good Nutrition Guidelines

To feel your best and stay healthy, follow these simple pieces of advice:

- Eat as many fruits and vegetables as possible. Sneak them in whenever you can—cut up fruit in your cereal or oatmeal, add veggies to your sandwich, eat them for snacks.
- Choose whole grains. Instead of white rice and white bread, pick brown rice and whole-wheat bread. Quinoa, oats, and barley are other examples of whole grains. They have more nutrients than non-whole grains.
- Vary your foods. Eat a variety of food every day to get as many nutrients as possible. Besides fruits, veggies, and grains, eat dairy and protein foods, like meat, beans, and nuts.
- Limit junk foods. Junk foods don't give you many nutrients, and they have unhealthy amounts of sugar and salt. You don't have to cut them out entirely, but save candy, cake, cookies, chips, soda, and other junk foods for special treats.
- Don't eat too much. Only eat when you're hungry, and only take as much food as you know you'll eat. Keep snacks between meals small so you'll be hungry for the actual meals.

Your Health

Healthy eating equals a healthy you. Your body works better when you feed it healthy foods.

All food gives you energy. Just like gas makes a car run, or batteries make a clock run, food makes human beings run. The healthiest foods give you the best energy and help you feel your best.

Some foods give you better energy than others. Healthy foods generally give you great energy. Fruits and vegetables, grains, dairy, and protein will give you energy that lasts for a while and gets you ready to do anything.

Sugar and caffeine are not great sources of energy. Have you ever eaten a lot of sugar and felt **jittery**? Pretty soon, the energy wears off, and then you just feel tired. Caffeine, which is a substance found in soda, coffee, tea, and chocolate, also provides temporary energy. It can also make you jittery and gets in the way of sleeping if you have too much caffeine late in the day.

In general, limit the junk food you eat. Junk foods are snacks that don't have much good stuff in them, like candy, cookies, and chips. You'll get small bursts of energy from them that wear off quickly.

You're better off sticking with long-lasting sources of energy rather than quick fixes like sugar. Long-lasting energy keeps you going for hours at a time. You'll be able to concentrate in school, play sports, and hang out with friends without getting really tired. Eating healthy foods will give you energy that feels good.

Healthy foods keep your **digestive system** working right too. And you'll avoid the headaches that come from eating too much sugar. You'll see better, have healthy bones, and have better skin.

Healthy eating also keeps you at a healthy weight. More and more young people are gaining weight, partly because of how they eat and partly because they aren't getting

What Does Jittery Mean?

When you are **jittery**, you are unable to relax, and you might feel like your body is shaking or tingling.

What Is the Digestive System?

The **digestive system** is what your body uses to break up and process food to make it into energy. Parts of the digestive system include the mouth, esophagus, stomach, and small and large intestines.

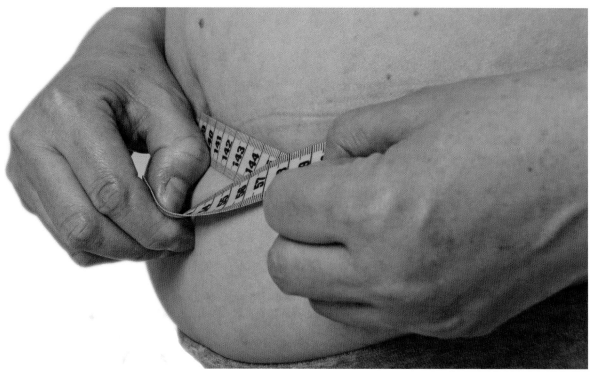

The food choices you make today can have an effect on your health for the rest of your life. Starting to make healthy choices now is the best way to stay healthy and in shape over time.

enough exercise. One in three young people are too heavy. Being **overweight** or **obese** leads to lots of health problems, both now and in the future. For example, even young people are getting diabetes now.

Diabetes is a disease in which the body doesn't use sugar correctly. People with diabetes must watch what they eat and get a lot of exercise. Over time, diabetes can cause even more health problems. In the past, mostly adults got diabetes. Today, as more young people gain weight, teenagers and even kids are getting diabetes.

What Do Overweight and Obese Mean?

When someone weighs a little too much, he is **overweight**. When someone is many pounds too heavy, she is **obese**. Obesity is a more extreme form of weighing too much.

Your Future

Your future health also depends on what you eat now. It's hard to think about what you'll be like ten, twenty, or more years in the future. But if you choose to eat healthy now, your future self will thank you.

Being overweight causes other health problem besides diabetes, including heart disease, stroke, kidney and liver disease, and even **cancer**.

Just because you eat right doesn't mean you won't have any health problems in the future. But healthy eating does lower your **risk** of getting them. Not only do you help yourself out right now by eating healthy, you also help your future self.

Moods and Emotions

Food affects your **emotional health**, just like it affects your physical health. Have you ever felt grumpy when you're hungry? Or felt really happy and energetic after eating a good meal? Food changes how you feel.

Eating regular meals will help keep your mood up. When people skip meals or get too hungry between meals, they often feel bad. They'll lose energy and feel physically bad, but they'll also be in a bad mood.

What Is Cancer?

Cancer is a disease that causes cells in your body to divide and grow faster than normal. These abnormal cells can make tumors that may grow larger and larger. The tumors can keep healthy cells and body organs from doing their jobs.

What Is a Risk?

A **risk** is the chance something unpleasant or dangerous will happen.

What Is Emotional Health?

Your **emotional health** is how well your mind is working. Good emotional health means you are generally happy and not worried or unhappy all the time.

FACTS FROM THE
AMERICAN DIABETES ASSOCIATION

Total: 25.8 million children and adults in the United States—8.3% of the population—have diabetes.

Diagnosed: 18.8 million people

Undiagnosed: 7.0 million people

Prediabetes: 79 million people

New Cases: 1.9 million new cases of diabetes are diagnosed in people aged 20 years and older in 2010.

Under 20 years of age:
215,000, or 0.26% of all people in this age group have diabetes. About 1 in every 400 children and adolescents has diabetes.

Diabetes is one of the many health problems that can be caused by making unhealthy food choices over time.

Some foods even put you in a good mood! Scientists have found that some foods help people who are feeling bad. Some of those foods include fish, fruits and vegetables, and foods with vitamin D in them, like cheese and eggs. Sugar, non-whole grains, and salt tend to make people feel worse.

Success

Healthy eating makes you feel good and helps your body work right. Good food choices can also help you do better at school, in sports, and more!

Scientists have shown that good nutrition can lead to better grades in school. Eating healthy food doesn't automatically make you smarter—but good nutrition does help you learn better.

When you eat healthy food and have a lot of energy, you can focus better in school. Instead of squirming around in your seat or daydreaming, you can pay attention to the teacher. You'll know what's going on in class.

You won't be falling asleep either. Skipping breakfast, for example, can make you really tired. Or you might be thinking about how hungry you are by 10:00 rather than thinking about class. If you had eaten a full, healthy breakfast, you would be paying better attention.

Good nutrition may also help with memory, so you can remember all the stuff you learn. When the test rolls around, you can clearly recall what you're supposed to know.

In sports, good nutrition is also really important. You can get sick if you don't eat enough of the right foods. When you play sports, you burn up a lot of energy. You have to replace the energy you lose by eating food. You don't want to just eat any food, though. Junk food isn't going to help you do better on the field. You want to eat healthy foods that will power you through practice or a game.

Anything you do will be better if you prepare for it by eating well. Music practice is easier, art class goes smoother, and you don't get too tired to go to the mall with friends. Even sleep will be easier with good nutrition!

Eating right and exercising can make you feel better and focus on the things that are important in your life. Making healthy food choices can lead to success in school, sports, and more.

More and more, as you get older, nutrition will be your choice. Even right now, you have plenty of chances to choose what kind of foods you eat. School cafeterias, vending machines, and convenience stores are just a few of those opportunities. They're places where you can choose to eat in a way that will make you stronger, healthier, and better at everything you do.

2

Choices
in the Cafeteria

You have a lot of choices that relate to food at school. You can eat breakfast at school or not. You can bring your lunch from home or buy it at school. You can skip lunch all together and wait to eat until you get home. You can eat a salad, pizza, or just french fries.

School cafeterias' choices vary from school to school. Some have healthier options than others. Whatever yours has on the menu, you can learn how to pick and choose what's really best for you.

Choosing to Eat Healthy

The school cafeteria is a convenient and sometimes necessary way to eat lunch. You don't have to remember to pack a lunch every day and carry it from home.

A lot of young people think of the cafeteria as a place to get an order of fries or a bag of chips. But the cafeteria can also give you a healthy meal that fills you up. Your goal is to choose foods with a lot of good nutrients.

Nutrients are substances in food that we need to eat for the body to work right. You're probably familiar with a couple kinds of nutrients—vitamins and minerals. Each vitamin and mineral helps your body work in a different way. Calcium keeps your bones strong. Iron carries oxygen in your blood to the **cells** in your body. Vitamin A helps you see well. Other vitamins and minerals do different things.

What Are Cells?

Cells are some of the tiniest parts of the human body. Everything in the body is made of cells; in fact, all living things are made out of cells. The brain is made out of brain cells, the skin is made out of skin cells, and the blood is made out of blood cells.

What Are Hormones?

Hormones are chemicals in the body that send messages to body parts to act in certain ways.

Other nutrients include carbohydrates. Sugar is a kind of carbohydrate. People need a little sugar every day, but not too much. Too much sugar leads to health problems. Sugar and the two other carbohydrates—fiber and starch—give us energy. We need carbohydrates to keep us going.

Protein is another nutrient. Protein also gives us energy, but it has a more important purpose. Protein keeps muscles strong, helps young people grow, and repairs cells.

Fat is another important nutrient. People need healthy fats for energy, and to protect organs and make **hormones**. Healthy fats are called unsaturated fats. Unhealthy fats also exist, called saturated and trans fats. You should limit how much unhealthy fat you eat.

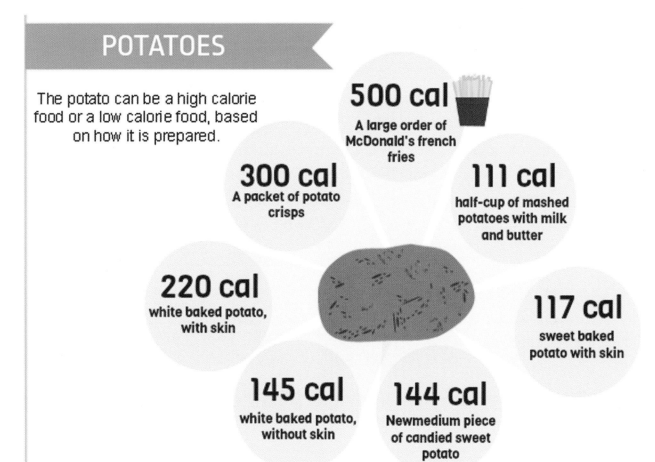

POTATOES

The potato can be a high calorie food or a low calorie food, based on how it is prepared.

500 cal A large order of McDonald's french fries

300 cal A packet of potato crisps

111 cal half-cup of mashed potatoes with milk and butter

220 cal white baked potato, with skin

117 cal sweet baked potato with skin

145 cal white baked potato, without skin

144 cal Newmedium piece of candied sweet potato

Potatoes are usually a healthy food choice. Fatty, salty potato chips or french fries aren't nearly as healthy as a baked potato.

Your school cafeteria can give you plenty of good nutrients if you know what to look for and what to avoid. First, look for fruits and vegetables. When you order a burger, add tomatoes and lettuce and onion. Go for the salad bar and load up on veggies. Get sides of fresh fruit and vegetables. Fruits and vegetables are healthy because they have a lot of those healthy nutrients.

If your cafeteria serves whole grains, definitely choose them! Whole grains are healthier than non-whole grains. Whole grains have more nutrients in them, like protein. Whole-wheat bread, whole-wheat pasta, and brown rice are all whole grains. White bread, white rice, and regular pasta are not whole grains.

Grilled foods are good choices (and avoid fried foods). Choose grilled chicken sandwiches, grilled veggie burgers, and salads with grilled mushrooms. Baked choices are also great, like baked fish, chicken, or tofu. Stir fries are a third good choice.

Choose milk, water, or 100 percent fruit juice to drink. If you drink milk, stick with plain milk instead of chocolate, strawberry, or another flavor. Flavored milks tend to have tons of sugar in them. Juice is another good choice, but only if it's 100 percent fruit juice, which means that all that's in there is fruit and water. A lot of "fruit" juices are mostly added sugar.

Making Changes

To transform an unhealthy lunch into a healthy one, just make a few changes. Instead of regular pizza, choose pizza with whole wheat crust and extra vegetables. Instead of french fries, choose a salad or baked sweet potato fries. Instead of soda, drink milk or water. And instead of ice cream for dessert, get a piece of fresh fruit.

Foods to Avoid

Lots of school cafeterias have some unhealthy food choices. You might be tempted to choose them for lunch, but challenge yourself to eat something healthier.

What's a Staple?

A **staple** is a main important part of a diet.

Pizza is a **staple** in most lunchrooms. Do you find yourself eating pizza for lunch almost every day? Limit yourself to pizza once a week. See if you can find some substitutes for it.

Lunch

TUNA SALAD SANDWICH ON WHOLE WHEAT BREAD — 215 CALORIES
GRILLED CHICKEN WRAP — 250 CALORIES
GRILLED SALMON SALAD — 300 CALORIES
PIZZA (2 SLICES) — 540 CALORIES
* BURGER, FRIES, SODA (SMALL MEAL) — 839 CALORIES

Junk foods like pizza, fries, and soda have many more calories than healthier food choices like a sandwich or salad. They're also filled with sugar, fat, and salt that can all lead to health problems if eaten too often.

Fried foods are also common in many school cafeterias. Maybe your cafeteria serves french fries every day. Or maybe it serves chicken nuggets, fish sticks, or onion rings. Fried foods are okay to eat once in a while, but you shouldn't eat them every day. Fried foods are full of unhealthy fats and salt, which are both bad for your health if you eat too much of them.

The other big category of food to limit is sugary food. Cafeterias often serve sugary foods because they know young people like them. Ice cream, cookies, flavored milk, and soda are all common. Too much sugar, though, is not good for learning. Foods with lots of sugar also don't usually have much else in them. There aren't enough good nutrients like vitamins and minerals in cookies or soda.

Real Cafeteria Recipes

Let's Move, the government's program to get young people making healthy choices, came up with a contest. The program challenged cafeterias around the country to come up with new, healthy, and tasty recipes students would love. Here are some of the winning recipes:

- Porcupine Sliders: turkey burgers shaped into balls, mixed with veggies and brown rice, and served on a whole-wheat bun.
- Crunchy Hawaiian Chicken Wrap: A whole-grain wrap with baked chicken, pineapple, spinach, and a sweet-and-sour sauce.
- Confetti Soup: A soup with all sorts of vegetables, herbs, and beans.
- Lentils of the Southwest: Lentils (a kind of seed similar to beans) mixed up with tomatoes, onions, and taco spices.

Watch out what you use for sauces and dressings. Mayonnaise-based dressings like ranch and cream-based sauces like alfredo aren't the best choices. Pick Italian dressing, mustard, marinara, and BBQ sauce instead.

New Choices in the Lunchroom

The U.S. government just passed a new law that changes what you eat in your school cafeteria. The new law says cafeterias have to serve healthier food.

What does that mean? Cafeterias have had to change a few things to follow the law. They can only serve fat-free or one-percent milk to cut down on how much fat students get every day. Every student must have at least a little bit of fruit or vegetables on their plate. More vegetables like kale are appearing on menus. New school lunches have limits on fat, and cafeteria foods have to have a lot of nutrients like vitamins and minerals.

According to the new law, all students must have at least three different **food groups** on their plate to buy lunch. Someone could have a hamburger on a whole-wheat bun with peaches on the side (fruit, grain, and protein) or brown rice with broccoli and a glass of milk (grain, vegetable, dairy).

The goal of this rule is to help students get a variety of foods. By eating lots of different foods from different food groups, you get a lot of different nutrients. Every food group has a different mix of nutrients. By eating every food group, you get all those nutrients, which makes your body work the way it should.

School meals will also have a new limit on calories. Calories are how people measure how much energy is in food. A food with 50 calories will give you a little bit of energy. A food with 150 calories will give you more energy. And a food with 500 calories will give you a lot of energy.

People need calories to live. Our bodies use up calories to do everyday things like walk, talk, and pump blood. Without calories, we would die.

However, people can also eat too many calories. When you eat too many calories, you start to gain weight. That's exactly what's happening to people today. Young people often overeat at school—and more and more young people are gaining weight.

The government is trying to stop some of that weight gain. Now, schools can't serve meals that are huge. For kindergarten through fifth grades, meals should be 650

What Are Food Groups?

Food groups are sets of foods that have similar nutrients. The five main food groups we usually talk about are fruits, vegetables, grains (wheat, rice, oats, quinoa, barley, and more), dairy (milk, yogurt, cheese), and protein (meat, nuts, beans, tofu).

Calorie Controversy

Some young people, teachers, and administrators are fighting against the new government school lunch law. They feel that the new calorie limits aren't high enough. For athletes and other students who need to eat a lot of calories, a 650-, 700-, or 850-calorie lunch just isn't enough. Some students are left hungry. If you're concerned about not getting enough food for lunch, talk to a teacher or your principal, who can help you figure out what to do next.

calories or less. For grades six through eight, meals are 700 calories or less. And for grades nine through twelve, meals are 850 calories or less.

Bringing Lunch from Home

For some kids, bringing lunch from home is a choice. Packed lunches can be healthier than school lunches if you pack the right things. If you don't like your school's food, or if you want even more healthy choices, bringing lunch from home might be the answer.

Bringing food from home lets you eat your favorite healthy foods. Do you love carrots and hummus but you can't find them at school? Bring them with you! Or maybe your school only serves peanut butter and jelly sandwiches on white bread. Bring a peanut-butter-and-jelly sandwich on whole-wheat bread from home.

Make sure your lunch from home has plenty of fruits and vegetables in it. Bring whole apples, bananas, oranges, or kiwis. Cut up carrots, celery, and broccoli. Bring whole grains, like sandwiches on whole-wheat bread and brown-rice dishes.

Eat a few different food groups. To get dairy, drink some milk or bring a yogurt (just make sure it doesn't have a ton of sugar in it). For protein, bring lunch meat, a handful of nuts, some bean soup, or a rice and bean burrito. Check out recipe books or recipe websites for some good packed lunch ideas.

From Blah to Healthy

Here's how you can transform your packed lunch. Instead of a bologna sandwich on white bread with mayonnaise, bring a turkey sandwich on whole-wheat bread with mustard, lettuce, and tomatoes. Instead of a bag of chips, bring air-popped popcorn, whole-wheat pretzels, or some veggies and dip. Instead of canned peaches, bring a fresh peach. Instead of a cookie for dessert, bring some trail mix or a whole-grain muffin with dried fruit. And instead of a fruit drink or soda, bring milk or 100 percent fruit juice.

Bringing your own lunch to school is a great way to make sure you're eating healthy foods.

Don't use packed lunches as an excuse to bring junk food! And don't trade away your healthy foods for junk food. Hang on to what you have and eat a filling lunch that will give you energy for the rest of your day.

Breakfast Choices

Most schools offer breakfast for students, along with lunch. Here again, you can make healthy and not-so-healthy choices in the cafeteria.

Nutrition Facts

Serving Size 1 container (227g)

Amount Per Serving

Calories 240 Calories from Fat 25

	% Daily Value*
Total Fat 3g	4 %
Saturated Fat 1.5g	9 %
Trans Fat 0g	
Cholesterol 15mg	5 %
Sodium 140mg	6 %
Total Carbohydrate 46g	15 %
Dietary Fiber Less than 1g	3 %
Sugars 44g	
Protein 9g	
Vitamin A 2 % • Vitamin C	4 %
Calcium 35 % • Iron	0 %

*Percent Daily Values are based on a 2,000 calorie diet. Your Daily Values may be higher or lower depending on your calorie needs.

When you bring a lunch from home, you can check the food labels on the foods you're packing for lunch and make sure you're not eating more salt, sugar, or fat than you need.

FRUITS

Fruits are generally low calorie foods. Fruit and vegetables should make up more than 2 thirds of your daily allowance. Fruit is so plentiful, is delicious to eat and there is such a wide variety, surely there is more than one type that will suit everyone's taste.

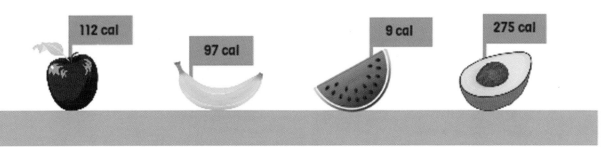

112 cal

97 cal

9 cal

275 cal

= **42 cal, but** a single cup of peaches in syrup = **194 cal.**

An average sized peach

Fruit is one of the healthiest food choices you can make, but remember that a fruit cup or canned fruit is not as healthy as eating a fresh piece of fruit.

Try to eat some fruits and whole grains. Oatmeal with fruit on top covers both. Eat a banana, an apple, or a smoothie if your school offers them. Take whole-wheat toast with peanut butter or real-fruit jelly. You have plenty of other good choices too. Eggs have protein and other good nutrients.

Breakfast is one meal where you might eat way too much sugar. Doughnuts, pastries, and some cereals—all of them have more sugar than you need. Avoid choosing those sugar-filled breakfasts all the time. It's okay to eat them once in a while, but limit them to once a week or even less.

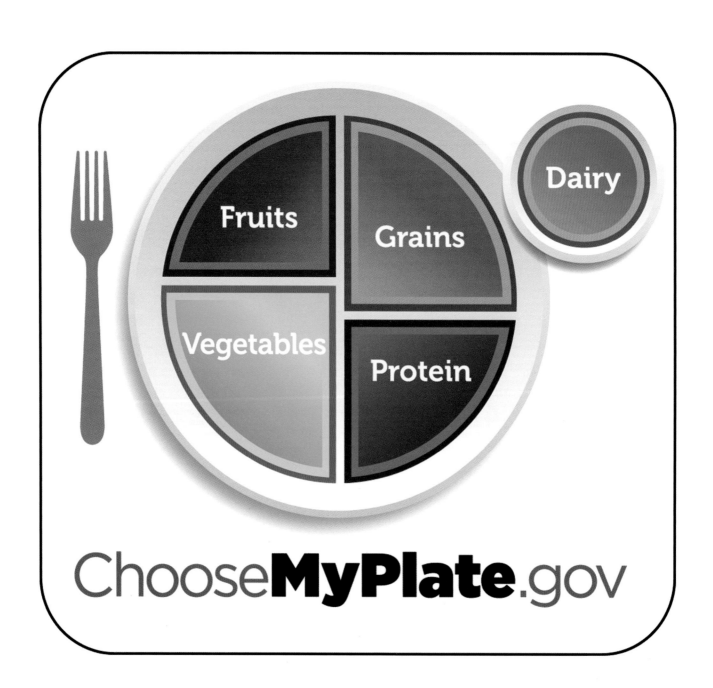

Getting enough of each of the main food groups is very important to balanced, healthy eating. Governments around the world share information about healthy eating with their people in different ways. This chart from the U.S. government gives you a sense of how much of each group you should be eating.

How to Make the Choice

When faced with the choice of either french fries or an apple, a lot of students will choose the fries. How are you supposed to stick to eating healthy when you want to choose the unhealthy foods?

First you have to make up your mind you want to eat healthy. You have so many good reasons: feeling better, being in a better mood, having enough energy for the school day, doing better at school and after-school activities.

At first, you might think eating healthier is hard. You're just not used to thinking about how to choose food that's healthy.

Maybe you even think healthy food tastes bad. It's okay not to like certain foods, but you have to keep an open mind. Give each food a chance. Don't just **assume** you'll hate a food because it's healthy. Maybe you think you hate broccoli. But have you ever had broccoli? Even if you have, your tastes might have changed. If you eat broccoli again and think, "Maybe I'll like this," you just might! Scientists say you need to try new foods a bunch of times before you know whether you like them or not.

Take small steps. Choose a healthy food to eat once a day. At lunch, you could choose a piece of fruit or some stir-fried carrots for lunch instead of french fries. You could pick out the 100 percent apple juice instead of soda. Congratulate yourself on making the healthy choice.

As you get used to making healthy choices, they'll get easier. Pretty soon, it won't be a chore. Healthy food choices will just be something you do automatically.

Don't be hard on yourself if you slip up once in a while. You'll be fine if you eat an Oreo or a bag of chips every now and then. Nothing bad will happen. The problems happen when you eat Oreos and chips every

What Does Assume Mean?

To **assume** means to automatically have an opinion about something, without thinking about it. You can assume a class will be hard or a food will be gross. But until you take the class or eat the food, you don't really know if your opinion is right or not.

Making healthy food choices in the cafeteria can help you stay healthy, do better in school, and feel better about yourself.

day. So go ahead and eat some cake for your friend's birthday, and enjoy the occasional order of french fries, as long as you don't go overboard.

Breakfast or lunch, you can be in control!

Farm-to-School Lunches

Some schools are working with local farms to get fresh ingredients for lunches. Sometimes the food in cafeterias has been shipped from across the country or the other side of the world. It doesn't taste so great because it's not very fresh. When cafeterias get vegetables, fruit, and meat from farms, though, food is very fresh. The ingredients come from just down the road, or the next town over. Farm-to-school programs often get students involved in picking ingredients and recipes. And lunches are much tastier, so students are more excited about eating healthy meals.

If you think this sounds like a good idea, talk to your parents and teachers to get ideas about what you could do to bring farm-to-school lunches to your cafeteria.

3
Spending Wisely, Staying Healthy

T he school cafeteria isn't always the only place to eat at school. Your school may have vending machines. There may be a convenience store across the street where you stop before and after school, or during your lunch period. It's up to you how you spend your money at these places.

Junk Food Galore

Students who don't like the food served in the cafeteria often go to a nearby convenience store. Some schools have their own convenience stores. These might also donate some

French Fries
29 lbs

Pizza
23 lbs

Ice Cream
24 lbs

Soda
53 gallons
(about a
gallon/week)

**Artificial
Sweeteners**
24 lbs

Sodium
2.736 lbs
(47% more than
recommended)

This chart shows the average amounts of junk foods, artificial sweetners, and sodium that Americans eat each year. It adds up! The average American eats around 2,700 calories a day when most people need between 1,500 and 2,000.

of their **profits** to one school class, or to the band or a sports team. Students want to go there to support their class or see their friends who are behind the counter.

The problem with most convenience stores is that they mostly sell junk foods. Junk foods are snacks with a lot of salt, sugar, or unhealthy fat. They don't have much good nutrition—that's why they're called junk.

Cookies, chips, ice cream, and more are all junk foods. Unfortunately, these are also many young peoples' favorite foods!

Junk food has empty calories. This means they have a lot of calories, but good nutrients, like protein or vitamins, don't come along with the calories. Instead, the calories are paired with too much salt, sugar, and unhealthy fat.

Salt, or sodium as it's called in nutrition, is good for people in small amounts. Sodium balances how much water is in the body. Too much sodium, though, can leave people **bloated**. Over time, too much sodium causes heart problems.

Next, unhealthy fats (which are called saturated and trans fats) also cause health problems. Unhealthy fats are found in fried things and junk foods. Too much unhealthy fat causes **cardiovascular** problems and can lead to heart attacks.

What Are Profits?

The people running a store first have to pay for running the store. They must give money to people working at the store, and pay to buy the things the store sells. Any money left over after that are the **profits**.

What Does Feeling Bloated Mean?

When people say they feel **bloated**, they meant that their bodies feel puffy and swollen. They feel like they're suddenly fatter than they really are. Their clothes may fit more tightly than usual, or the rings on their fingers may be tighter.

What Does Cardiovascular Mean?

Cardiovascular refers to the body system made up of the heart and blood vessels.

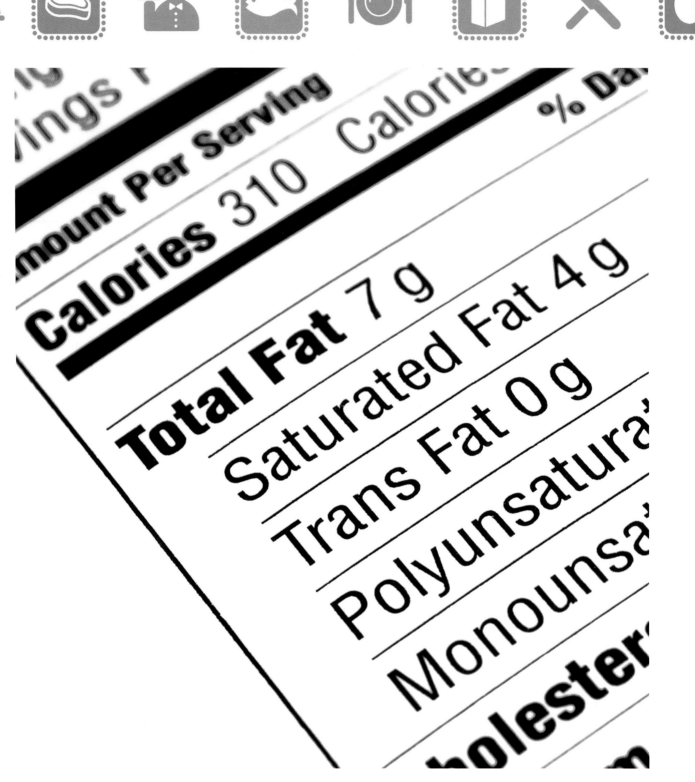

Calories 310

Total Fat 7 g

Saturated Fat 4 g

Trans Fat 0 g

Make sure to check the nutrition facts on the foods you buy at the convenience store. Food labels let you know how many calories are in the food you're buying, as well as how much fat, sugar, and salt the foods are made with. Checking these labels can help you make healthier food choices.

Finally, sugar is in just about all junk foods these days. When you look at the list of ingredients on many snack food packages, you'll usually see words like high-fructose corn syrup, corn syrup, fructose, dextrose, glucose, and sucrose. These are all more words for sugar. Sugar gets **addictive**, so once you start eating sugar, you want more! People need some sugar, but most of us eat too much. Too much sugar causes headaches and loss of energy. Over time, it leads to a higher risk of weight gain, diabetes, heart disease, and more.

Junk food has all three of these dangerous ingredients. Eating junk food once in a while won't hurt you. When you go to the convenience store to buy them every day, though, you're doing yourself more harm than good.

What Does Addictive Mean?

When something is **addictive**, you want to enjoy it all the time in an extreme and unhealthy way. People get addicted to drugs, computer games, gambling, and food. People who are addicted to drugs, for example, have to have their drug of choice to feel calm and happy.

Convenience Store Dos and Don'ts

When you buy food at the convenience store, you'll need to sift through what's there to get a healthy snack.

In general, don't get your lunch from the school store. Unless they sell healthy lunch choices like whole-wheat sandwiches with veggies, you're better off sticking with the cafeteria. Try new things in the cafeteria, or try the salad bar line. Bring your lunch from home if you can. The cafeteria will fill you up and keep you going, unlike junk food from the convenience store.

Choose carefully when you're buying something from a convenience store. Instead of automatically choosing chips and a soda, take your time. Try out that new kind of granola bar with almonds and coconut. Choose the fruit juice or some water, not the soda.

Sugary drinks can have many more calories in them than you might expect. Sometimes a single serving of these drinks can have more than 200 calories!

Keep junk food purchases to special occasions. Try not to eat junk foods every single day. Keep it to once a week or less, and your body will thank you.

Maybe your store sells fresh fruit. Even if you get chips or cookies, get a piece of fruit too. That way, you're eating something healthy, even if you're also eating junk food.

Vending Machines

Vending machines are another way you can fill up on junk food. When you're looking for a quick snack between classes or a pick-me-up after school, you might turn to a vending machine.

The problem with many vending machines is that they mostly or only have unhealthy foods in them. Drink machines have soda and sports drinks that are filled with sugar. Snack machines have ice cream bars, salty chips, cookies, and Pop Tarts®.

None of those things are really going to fill you up and give you long-lasting energy. And eating too many of them leads to weight gain and health problems.

Vending machines make grabbing a quick drink easy when you're on the go, but drinking soda too often can lead to weight gain and health problems.

When you have money to spend on food, it's important to take the time to think about the kind of food you're buying. When you shop for yourself, you have to make healthy food choices on your own.

Take Action!

Do you care a lot about eating healthy food and want better options at school? More and more schools are realizing the importance of good nutrition, but some are still not offering enough good choices. If you're worried about what your school store, vending machines, or cafeteria is selling, speak up! Talk to your student council, the school newspaper, a teacher, the school nurse, the principal, or the school board. Talk to as many people as you can. Someone will listen and help you figure out how to start getting healthier food choices at school.

Depending on your school, you might actually have some healthy choices in your vending machines. Some schools have decided to do away with soda, cookies, and more in favor of healthier things. Then your choice isn't so hard. You can't reach for the packaged cakes because they're not there! Instead, you can choose from packs of baby carrots and dip, 100 percent fruit juice, baked chips with less salt, and granola bars.

Look for the best choices in vending machines. Anything that says whole wheat, like whole-wheat pretzels, is a better choice. Baked chips, low-salt snacks, and granola bars without a lot of sugar tend to be good choices too.

If you don't have healthy vending machine options (or healthy convenience store choices), what should you do? You can always plan ahead. Bring some snacks from home with you. You know you always get hungry between breakfast and lunch, so bring some trail mix or a piece of fruit or whatever healthy snack you'd like. Then you won't even have to go to the machines.

Going Out For Lunch

Some high schools allow students to walk or drive to lunch places nearby. You'll have a lot more freedom during lunch. And you'll also be faced with a whole new set of food

Eating fatty foods and sugary sodas sometimes isn't bad, but making healthier food choices more often is the best way to stay healthy as you get older.

decisions. You could go to Burger King® and get a burger and French fries every day. Or you could head to a salad bar or sandwich shop with veggie options. It's up to you!

Use what you know about good nutrition to make good choices. You'll be making the same choices as you do in the cafeteria, with the same knowledge. Limit fried foods, choose fruits and vegetables and whole grains. Stay away from junk food.

Your Money, Your Choice

As you get older, you'll have more and more choices. Right now, one of the biggest choices you have is what you eat. And when you have some money, that choice is even more important.

Do you want to spend your money on something that will make you feel bad and get sick? Or do you want to spend your money on something that will make you feel great and will help you stay strong and healthy?

Find Out More

Online

KidsHealth: School Lunches
www.kidshealth.org/kid/homework/lunch/school_lunches.html#cat119

Let's Move!
www.letsmove.gov

Nourish Interactive
www.nourishinteractive.com

In Books

Claybourne, Anna. *Healthy Eating: Diet and Nutrition.* Mankato, Minn.: Heinemann-Raintree, 2008.

Curtis, Andrea. *What's for Lunch? How Schoolchildren Eat Around the World.* Markham, Ontario: Red Deer Press, 2012.

Wagner, Lisa. *Cool Lunches to Make and Take.* Minneapolis, Minn.: Abdo Publishing Company, 2007.

Index

breakfast 9, 15, 19, 28–29, 33, 43

cafeteria 7, 19–25, 28, 32–33, 35, 39, 43–45
caffeine 11
calories 7, 23, 25–26, 36–38, 40
carbohydrates 20

dairy 10–11, 25–26
diabetes 12–14, 37

energy 10–11, 13, 15, 20, 25, 28, 31, 37, 41

farms 33
fat 7, 20–21, 23, 25, 28, 37–39, 44
food groups 25–26, 30
fried foods 7, 22–23, 45
fruits 7, 10–11, 15, 21–22, 25–27, 29, 31, 33, 39–41, 43, 45

grains 7, 10, 11, 15, 21–22, 24–27, 29, 45

heart disease 13, 37

junk food 10–11, 23, 37, 39, 40

minerals 20, 24, 25
money 35, 37, 42, 45

nutrients 10, 20–21, 24–25, 29, 37
nutrition 3, 6–7, 9–10, 15, 37–38, 43, 45–46

packed lunch 26–28
protein 7, 10–11, 20, 25–26, 29, 37

recipes 24, 33

salt 10, 15, 21, 23, 28, 37–38, 41, 43
school store 39, 43
snacks 10, 11, 37, 43, 45
soda 7, 10–11, 22–24, 27, 31, 39, 41, 43–44
sports 6, 9, 11, 15–16, 37, 41
sugar 10, 12–15, 20, 22–24, 26, 28–29, 37–38, 40–44

vegetables 7, 10–11, 15, 21–22, 24–26, 33, 45
vending machines 17, 35, 41, 43
vitamins 15, 20, 24–25, 37

weight 6, 11–13, 25, 37, 41
weight gain 25, 37, 41
whole wheat 10, 22, 24–27, 29, 39, 43

About the Author & Consultant

Kyle A. Crockett is a freelance writer whose work can be found in print and online. His writing for young people has focused on topics ranging from health to economics.

Dr. Borus graduated from the Harvard Medical School and the Harvard School of Public Health. He completed a residency in Pediatrics and then served as Chief Resident at Floating Hospital for Children at Tufts Medical Center before completing a fellowship in Adolescent Medicine at Boston Children's Hospital. He is currently an attending physician in the Division of Adolescent and Young Adult Medicine at Boston Children's Hospital and an Instructor of Pediatrics at Harvard Medical School.

Picture Credits